To Zahira, with love, David & ...

GW01464280

TWO BEARS
find a pet

Story by Cathie and David Bell

Pictures by Jan Brychta

Oxford University Press

For Emily

Oxford University Press, Walton Street, Oxford OX2 6DP

Oxford   New York   Toronto
Delhi   Bombay   Calcutta   Madras   Karachi
Petaling Jaya   Singapore   Hong Kong   Tokyo
Nairobi   Dar es Salaam   Cape Town
Melbourne   Auckland

and associated companies in
Berlin   Ibadan

Oxford is a trade mark of Oxford University Press

© Oxford University Press 1990
Printed in Hong Kong

A CIP catalogue record for this book is available from the
British Library.

The Two Bears Books are:

Two Bears at the seaside
Two Bears in the snow
Two Bears at the party
Two Bears go fishing
Two Bears find a pet
Two Bears and the fireworks

Winston and Stanley went to the school fair.
In the playground there were lots of stalls
and rides.

Winston saw a big cake on one of the stalls.
There was a poster which said:
'Guess the weight and win the cake!'
Stanley had one guess, but Winston really wanted
to win so he had twenty-three guesses.

And Winston won!
'Well done!' said the headteacher. 'Next week
we're having our Pet Show. So if you have a pet,
do bring it along.'

When Winston and Stanley got home they had
tea and a slice of cake.
Winston was thinking.
'I do wish we had a pet,' he said.

That night, Winston had a dream.
He and Stanley got a giraffe from the pet shop.
But the giraffe was too tall to go in the
front door.

Then he dreamed he had a hippopotamus.
But the hippopotamus sat in the bath all day
and wouldn't come out.

Last of all, he dreamed he had a lion.
But the lion was so fierce that the bears
were frightened to go near it.

Next morning, Winston told Stanley about his dreams.
'We can't have animals like that,' said Stanley.
'We need a small pet — one that's easy to look after.'
Then they saw the cake . . .

Someone had been eating it!
'It wasn't me,' said Winston.
'It wasn't me, either,' said Stanley.
There was a line of crumbs across the floor.

The two bears followed the line.
There was a tiny mouse in a corner of the room.
It had a big piece of cake between its paws.

Stanley picked up the mouse.
'This is just the pet for us,' he said.

They called the mouse Clementine.
They took her for walks in the park and showed her
how to do tricks.

When the day of the Pet Show came,
Winston and Stanley took Clementine
to the Best Pet Competition.
She did a cartwheel and won first prize!

The two bears were very pleased.
'She's the best pet in the world,' they said.